LION KING COLLECTIBLES
Lisa Courtney

AMBERLEY

Acknowledgements

The author would like to thank the following for their assistance with some of the photos in this book: Chiara Carchidio, Derek Cooling, Heather Ann Airdrie, Manon Bouwens, Lauren Williamson and Marie Dussol. Special shout outs to Cornelius and Xemnas for not breaking anything while I was working on this book, and to my mother, for putting up with my collecting habits for all these years and assisting me with the photos. I love you, you're the greatest.

First published 2019

Amberley Publishing
The Hill, Stroud
Gloucestershire, GL5 4EP

www.amberley-books.com

Copyright © Lisa Courtney, 2019

The right of Lisa Courtney to be identified as the Author of this work has been asserted in accordance with the Copyrights, Designs and Patents Act 1988.

ISBN 978 1 4456 9575 4 (print)
ISBN 978 1 4456 9576 1 (ebook)

British Library Cataloguing in Publication Data. A catalogue record for this book is available from the British Library.

Typeset in 10pt on 13pt Celeste.
Typesetting by Aura Technology and Software Services, India. Printed in the UK.

Contents

Introduction

In the year 1988, development began on a movie that was viewed as nothing more than another animated animal tale from Walt Disney. With Disney's top animators choosing to work on *Pocahontas*, another Disney movie being concurrently produced, the company had little faith that *The Lion King* would be anything more than moderately successful.

To Disney's surprise, in 1994 *The Lion King* was unleashed to the world and became a roaring success at the box office. Featuring stunning animation, a memorable cast, catchy African-styled tunes and an engaging story, the movie went on to become the highest-grossing release of 1994, the highest-grossing traditionally animated movie and the best-selling film on home video, with over 30 million tapes sold across the world. From here, the movie spanned sequels, spin-offs and even a Broadway musical, which became the highest-grossing Broadway show of all time.

When it comes to *The Lion* King, there are many different types of collectors in the world, with many different focuses. Some choose to collect their favourite character, others a specific type of collectible, such as figures or plush toys. There are also those who, like me, just enjoy collecting whatever they can. However, the merchandise that has been released for *The Lion King* and its sequels and spin-offs is a vast realm. As such, this book is not a complete encyclopaedia of every *Lion King* item ever released, but a guide to some of the more desirable and interesting collectibles pertaining to the franchise, encompassing as many different collectible types as possible. We'll be straying away from some merchandise lines that cross realms and are already well documented elsewhere (Funko Pops, pin badges, Tsum Tsums, etc.) and mostly keeping to merchandise obtainable in the UK and Europe, though there are a few exceptions to these rules here and there. I hope that this book will rekindle some fond memories, or, for those new to collecting *The Lion King* memorabilia, I hope that this will offer some insight into the world of *Lion King* collectibles.

Chapter One
The Lion King

The year was 1994, and a new Disney movie hit the cinemas. To Disney, this film was to be just another movie under their belt, nothing more than a little extra pocket money for the company. Little did anyone know that this new movie would be one of their most popular films, reach record-breaking sales and capture the heart of millions around the world for years to come. Prince Simba's journey from young cub to rightful king evoked many emotional reactions from its audience, and cemented its place as one of the greatest animated films of all time, spawning a wide variety of collectibles over a period of nearly twenty-five years.

With some merchandise relating to the first movie, it's possible to determine roughly what year it was produced in by examining the packaging. The earliest merchandise, first released in 1994, feature clusters of green foliage and use the original logo with the sun rising in the background. In 2003, the pattern resembled the opening of the movie, with a red-orange background and a white logo in a brown box. Merchandise released during the Diamond Edition Blu-ray release typically featured golden text with a blue sky overlooking the African plains, often with an image of Simba looking to his left or right. This isn't true to all merchandise, however, since some companies took a different approach.

At the movie's initial release, Mattel was the primary licence holder for merchandise. What are arguably the most well-known collectibles stem from their toy lines. Other popular lines are Jemini, Applause and Douglas.

Packaging examples, featuring Spectra Star Simba yo-yo, Energizer Pumbaa light and Just Play Zazu and Scar flocked figures.

Assorted *Lion King* figures

Figures are very popular with *Lion King* collectors. There are many different figures out there from many companies. Shown here from left to right are: Disney Rafiki, Bullyland Simba, Mattel toddler Simba, Burger King Zazu, Christmas cracker Nala, flocked talking Simba keychain, Tomy Pumbaa, Disney Store Classics Timon and Pumbaa figure, Disney Special Edition Banzai figure and Simba and Scar chess pieces.

Boxed Mattel figures

A set of collectible figures were among the first items on the market. These durable plastic figures often used very distinct models that were not reproduced for future markets, and included some more realistic animal models based on the creatures that gathered for Simba's presentation during Circle of Life. (Photography by Derek Cooling)

Prototype Mattel figures
Prototypes of these figures also exist. As is to be expected, they rarely pop up. This collection of prototype figures belongs to Chiara Carchidio. The figure of Mufasa carrying Simba was unfortunately never released to the public. (Photography by Chiara Carchidio)

Mattel figures – Mufasa and Simba, Sarabi, Pumbaa and Scar
These models are highly collectible to fans, even out of their original packaging. Sarabi is one of the most sought-after figures for collectors due to her overall lack of merchandise throughout the years.

Mattel action figure gift set
The action figure line is similarly well known to fans. The figures could be purchased in bubble-backed cards, though a selection of figures were also released in a box set, which included some accessories. (Photography by Derek Cooling)

Pride Rock Playset
Accompanying these figures was the Pride Rock playset, which is another staple for many collectors. Although no figures are included, some skeletal accessories for the elephant graveyard portion of the playset were included instead. (Photography by Derek Cooling)

Jungle Babies Sleeping Simba and Snacking Simba
Another toy line is the Jungle Babies set, which, as their name suggests, featured baby figures of certain characters. Some of these figures have a special trick, such as these two: Snacking Simba opens his mouth to eat or to drink from a little bottle, and Sleeping Simba closes his eyes when he's laid down.

Boxed Just Play figures and unboxed Mattel figures
For the Diamond Edition release, Just Play took over the main figure line. However, many of their larger products bear a striking resemblance to the original Mattel models. In this picture, the Mattel figures are shown out of their box and the Just Play figures are shown in box.

Disneyland Resort Paris figure set
This figure set, including Simba, Nala, Scar, Zazu, Rafiki, Timon, Pumbaa and Nala, could be found at Disneyland Paris. They aren't too difficult to find these days, mainly due to being in production for a very long time. They were later replaced with a similar set in a golden box.

The Lion King **box set**
This mini box set includes a book of the movie, plus figures of cub Simba, Mufasa, Rafiki, Timon and Pumbaa. The front of the box uses the same image from the book.

Magic Mates Simba
This voice-activated Simba was released back when electronic toys like these were popular. He will move his head around and say phrases like 'Do you wanna play hide and seek?', but the voice actor is not the original. Other Disney characters were also available to purchase.

The Lion King DVD Gift Set
This Special Edition DVD Gift Set includes a copy of *The Lion King* Special Edition, a Penguin book of the movie, a backdrop and six character figurines (Simba, Timon, Pumbaa, Scar, Banzai and Mufasa).

The Lion King Deluxe Figurine Playset
This Disney Store-exclusive figure set was released around the time of the Special Edition movie. As with many of these sets, the Scar and hyena figures are particularly desirable. It's easy to spot these figures loose, but difficult to locate them in this box.

Mattel Toddler Figures
Don't be fooled by the wording on the box! These soft figures by Mattel can be difficult to obtain, particularly in the original box. Sarabi is especially popular with collectors, and will fetch the highest price of all the original Toddler figures even unboxed. (Photography by Heather Ann Airdrie)

Above left: **Play Set Tub**
This tub included a playmat, figures and accessories. It was released in Disney Stores around the time of the Special Edition release. Finding the figures alone is not too much of a challenge, but finding them complete and still in the tub is a different story.

Above right: *Kingdom Hearts* **Simba and Requiem**
The *Kingdom Hearts* series was a huge success for both Disney and Square. In fact, Simba was the only reason I purchased the first game in the beginning, introducing me to one of my favourite video game series! This figure, which comes packaged with a Requiem, is made by Mirage and part of the second wave of this figure line.

Talk 'n' View Pond
After pressing the button, one of the characters featured on the box will light up and call out their catchphrase. Sometimes, you may find the attached Simba figure alone. A similar figure was also released in Canada, where Simba stands more upright.

Assorted *Lion King* plush toys

Plush toys are another popular choice for *Lion King* collectors. Shown is a random assortment of plush toys from various companies. The cub Simba and Nala are notable for being one of, if not the earliest plush toys of Simba and Nala available at Disneyland Paris, and a similar pattern was later reused for a Kiara plush at Disney on Ice. Meditating Rafiki is also a Disneyland Paris release, albeit a later one. Sarabi is another popular item and finding her with baby Simba can be a bit of a challenge. Timon is from Clintons and Pumbaa is by Applause. Zazu plus the Scar and Mufasa beanie are Disney Store releases, with Scar being from an earlier range. The adult Simba hot-water bottle plush is sometimes mistaken for being a bootleg, and it's not hard to see why – the colour is drastically different when compared to other plush toys from *The Lion King*. This isn't a common item to find, and it is almost always sold without the hot-water bottle and labelled instead as a pyjama case.

Mattel Baby Simba

Mattel also unleashed a variety of plush toys to the market. These early toys are quite distinct in comparison to the toys that are now produced, and are often recognised by their plastic eyes and overall design. (Photography by Manon Bouwens)

Plastic-headed Mattel plush toys
Another popular series, these plastic-headed plush toys were also among the first toys the public could purchase. The first wave consisted of Zazu, Rafiki, Shenzi, Timon and Pumbaa, but Mattel later released similar toys, such as a Simba with cheaper plush material.

Disney Store Simba (and Nala) plush toys
Yet another Disney Store exclusive, this particular Simba plush can be found in various sizes. The largest at 3 feet long and retailing for £60 is by far the rarest, and was produced in much smaller quantities. A matching Nala was also produced in the medium and small size range, and other materials, such as a scruffy material, were later produced in medium and small sizes. Shown from left to right: jumbo Simba, medium scruffy Simba, small Simba, beanie Nala.

Disney Store re-release plush toys
For the Diamond release, another batch of plush toys were created for Disney Stores. Shown here are the zebra, Simba, Nala, Zazu and Rafiki plush toys.

Hula Timon and Pumbaa plush toys
Are you achin' for some bacon? These small plush toys are perfect for you! Based off the iconic hula scene from the movie, these are Disney Store plush toys. Although the tag here reveals that these are the US-released toys, they were also purchasable in UK stores.

Giant Disneyland Paris Simba plush
This giant Simba measures nearly 2 feet, and was available for a short time during *The Lion King* Carnival at Disneyland Paris. Large plush toys such as these are popular with many collectors, despite taking up a lot of space.

Baby Simba plush toys
These are quite possibly some of the most popular affordable plush toys. They were released in the Disney Parks and some Disney Stores, and have been re-released many, many times. A quick way to distinguish roughly which release you have typically relies on inspecting the butterflies. The plushies here are laid out in order from earliest (left) to one of the most recent (right). A similar baby Simba plush, released in Walmart, features a purring mode and lacks the butterfly.

'Can't Wait to Be King' Limited Edition Simba plush
Limited to 3,500 pieces, this Simba plush was released exclusively at Disney Stores. He doesn't come with any type of certificate, however, much to the disappointment of many collectors.

Disney Store Scar plush toys
These three Scar plush toys are all Disney Store releases, but each one has a distinct difference. From left to right, a US-exclusive large Scar, the UK-released Scar, and the re-released Scar, which hit the shelves several years later.

Simba plush slippers, round Simba plush, and baby Simba pillow plush
For the people who want plush toys that are a little different, here are some excellent choices. The ball-like Simba is made by Nicotoy, the baby Simba pillow is made by Disneyland Paris, and the baby Simba slippers are made by Disney Store. According to the label, they're child size XL, or 32–34, but still seem to fit me despite my shoe size being 42.

Jumbo Mufasa plush
One of the most sought-after items by collectors, this jumbo-sized Mufasa plush was released at Disney Stores in the US, but could also be purchased online. The nearly 3-foot-tall king sold out quickly over there. There are rumours that he also appeared in the UK, but only at select stores, where he sold out almost immediately.

Baby Simba and Family, and Kissing Cubs Hasbro sets
These two Hasbro playsets were released to coincide with the release of the special edition. The sets contained two small plush toys, a figure and a small playset. Simba's mane can be removed.

Shenzi, Banzai and Ed Disney Store plush toys
The hyena trio are very popular for collectors. This set of plush toys, released by Disney Store in 2011, flew off the shelves upon release, and are very desirable items. They can be expensive when found in good condition, and frequently sell for upwards of £80 each.

Douglas plush toys
When it comes to *Lion King* collectibles, plush toys created by Douglas are high on a collector's wish list. These high-quality soft toys almost always reach high prices, even if the condition is poor. Some Douglas plush toys have sold for £500 upwards in the past. (Photography by Manon Bouwens)

Baby Simba and Baby Nala Disney Store beanies
These two beanies were released around the time of the Special Edition release. They were not on shelves for very long, making them sought-after plush toys.

Posh Paws Simba prototypes

You are very likely going to see a lot of variations on these plush toys, made by Posh Paws. They come in several sizes and plush materials, and even different boxes. The two shown to the right are prototype plush toys, and contain some minor differences to the final releases.

Simba frame plush toys

Plush toys carrying picture frames were a novelty item at Disney Stores for a few years. You can sometimes find the frames absent from the plush. The frames themselves are only plastic, so at least you don't have to worry about breaking any glass.

Three Kissing Cubs sets

Kissing Cubs plush toys are almost a tradition at this point. These toys have a magnetic nose so that the cubs can kiss, as their name suggests. Mattel released the first set of Kissing Cubs back when the original movie debuted. Giochi Preziosi released an updated set for the Diamond Edition release, and more recently, Disney Store created their own Kissing Cubs as part of their Valentine's Day range. These cubs not only kiss, but also make a sound when doing so.

Disney Parks Simba and Mufasa plush
This plush was found in various Disney Parks around the world. Simba is attached to his father.

Jemini plush Simba backpack
Jemini are another popular toy company, and their products are desirable to *Lion King* collectors. Shown here is a Simba plush backpack.

Scar and hyena trio salt and pepper shakers
These little ceramic figurines can be hard to track down, if only because Scar and the hyenas are just so popular for collectors.

The Lion King **storybook ornament set**
This set comes packaged in a rather extravagant storybook box, as the name suggests it would. It was also re-released in a different packaging.

25

Disney Classics 2007 mug

In the early days of the Disney Store, collectable mugs were extremely popular items, alongside snow globes. *The Lion King* saw its fair share of these mugs, which often contained very detailed and vibrant designs that are often sought after by many collectors.

Various Disney Classics mugs

The early boxes were rather standard, but later boxes included a lid. Shown above are the Classics 2010 and 2011 mugs, and below them are the Classics 2009 and 2006 mugs. These days, a wide variety of mugs are still manufactured, but most of them no longer come packaged in a box, nor do they have any specific date printed on them. However, this does not mean they are no longer popular.

Disney Store Simba plush in mugs

For several years, Disney Stores began a trend of releasing plush toys with their mugs, such as these. The plush toys are tied to the mug via a plastic clip, and sometimes are seated on a small piece of cardboard to elevate the plush to the top. Several of the plush look similar, but do have minor differences between them.

Disney Store plush in mugs (mini and regular sizes)

Most of the plush toys that came with the mugs were of cub Simba, but here is a rare example of baby Simba being used. The mini mug is also by Disney Store, although they haven't produced many of these collectable mini mugs.

Disney Store mugs
Mugs such as these are a common sight in Disney Stores across the world at present. While they no longer portray the movie scenes as their predecessors once did, their designs are still inviting.

Rafiki and Simba mugs
Finally, mugs such as these are very popular with collectors, and tend to sell out quickly at stores. Rafiki is part of an early series released for the original movie and is part of a set including adult Simba and Scar. When these come up for sale, they are usually expensive. The Simba mug is a more recent release from the Disney Store.

Disneyland Paris glass Simba ornaments
If you ever head off to Disneyland Paris, these glass ornaments make a wonderful souvenir. While the overall appearance often changes with time, they can usually be acquired on certain stores in Main Street. They're not cheap, but other characters are also available. Don't ask me which others though, I only search for *Lion King* items at the parks!

Simba garden gnome
This off-colour statue (which Woolworth's listed under the garden gnome section) stands at approximately 9.5 inches.

Ceramic Simba bank
This large ceramic Simba money bank is wonderful, but the paint is very flimsy. Extra care must be taken with this, since some of these have a problem with paint actually falling off in chunks.

Disney baby Simba lamp
Baby Simba is often used by Disney in their Disney Baby range. Products from this line can often be expensive, but the quality justifies the price tag. Such is the case with this baby Simba lamp.

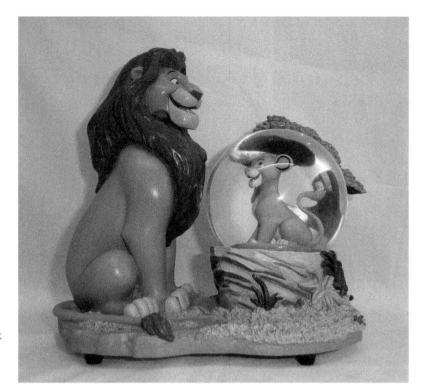

Mufasa and Simba snow globe
This snow globe features father and son. When wound up, a music box rendition of 'Circle of Life' will play.

Disneyland Paris mini snow globes
These two mini snow globes were both available at Disneyland Paris. The one with Simba and Nala is more recent.

31

Light-up snow globe
One of the larger snow globes, this beautiful collectible also plays a music box rendition of 'Circle of Life' when wound up. Mufasa's cloud also lights up.

Ceramic Simba figures
Smaller ceramic figures such as these are very light. I place mine towards the back of my shelves to avoid accidentally knocking them to the floor.

Lion King **Christmas ornaments**
Even now, the Disney Store frequently releases Christmas ornaments with a *Lion King* theme. These heavy collectibles tend to retire the same year. Another company that are quite keen on releasing *Lion King*-themed ornaments are Hallmark. In this image, the first two from the left are Disney Store releases, and the two from the right are Hallmark ornaments.

The Lion King Sega Mega Drive and Sega Master System games
Released for the Mega Drive (Genesis for those reading from the USA), Master System, Game Gear, Game Boy, SNES, NES, Amiga and PC/DOS, *The Lion King* is considered by some to be a very challenging game, partly due to the second level, 'The Mane Event'. I played my Mega Drive copy so much that the game now glitches at random intervals during gameplay and sends me back to Timon's 'It Starts'! Of all the releases, the PAL-exclusive NES version is considered to be the rarest, with it being the last officially released NES game ever made.

The Lion King board game
This game retells the story of the movie, with the penultimate goal of defeating Scar and reclaiming the throne. It was re-released for the Special Edition, in a plainer box.

Sounds of Fun board game

This board game, created by Parker Brothers, is somewhat difficult to locate complete. The game board itself is another 3D board, and features sounds from the cast.

The Lion King Adventures Sega Pico game

While the Sega Pico did not fare so well in the UK, that didn't stop *The Lion King* from getting a game on the platform before it was discontinued. The pages loosely follow cub Simba's story, omitting darker scenes such as the elephant graveyard and stampede.

The Lion King **puzzle selection**
Puzzles from a variety of companies have been made over the years. While 1,000-piece puzzles aren't too uncommon these days, back when *The Lion King* first came out they were very difficult to locate, with most puzzles being targeted towards children. This, coupled with age, makes the puzzle on the left one of the rarest *Lion King* puzzles.

The Lion King **Waterfuls**
In the 1990s, these toys were all the rage. Milton Bradley created a *Lion King*-themed edition of this game under the title of Waterfuls.

Jungle Heroes items – bags, plush, pins watch and lollipop
A Disneyland Paris exclusive series, the Jungle Heroes set featured many items and was primarily aimed at younger fans. Plates, cups, cutlery, colouring supplies, bags, a wallet, a lollipop and even a lucky bag (which contained a paper clip, pencil and topper, magnet and notepad) were all part of this series. All of these items have the Jungle Heroes logo printed somewhere on the items, either on the packaging or the item itself.

Jungle Heroes items – cutlery, stationery, lucky bag and wallet
In addition to these, a towel and children's apparel items were also available.

'The Legend of the Lion King' items

In 2004, Disneyland Paris began a new show inspired by *The Lion King*. Guests could obtain a ticket with a set time to return to watch the performance, either in English or French. Although not too much merchandise was created for the show specifically, these items could be purchased for a limited time in the parks (save for the park maps, which were free). A t-shirt and pin are also available.

Disney Store 'Sketch' series items

One of Disney Store's exclusives, this series – which I dub the Sketch series – includes a variety of unique items with sketch-like designs (hence the nickname). Of particular note is the golf set, an item not usually seen very often on the secondary market. Other items were also produced, such as a regular figure set and a towel.

Mufasa and Simba series items
Another Disney Store exclusive, this set was geared more towards adult fans and included more practical items such as a box of notelets and picture frame. With a simplistic yet charming design focusing on the main character and his father, these items were only available for a short time before they sold out in stores and online. Inside the mug at the bottom, Rafiki's portrait of young Simba can be found.

Nala series items
Another Disney Store series focused on Simba's childhood friend, Nala. It was released as part of a summer range. The small bag also came with glitter armbands and deflated beach ball attached. Not pictured are a towel, children's tutu set, and sunglasses.

Disney on Ice items
Disney on Ice is a popular ice skating show that frequently returns to the UK. Despite *The Lion King* being one of the more favoured portions of the show, merchandise is not all that common at the shows, and they often overlook *The Lion King* completely. Here are a few older items from the show: a Simba plush, programme, bookmark, t-shirt and flag.

Assorted *Lion King* cushions

Shown here is an assortment of cushions. The top one is double-sided, the one on the left comes with a Zazu plush in a pocket and was available to buy at Disneyland Paris. The other two are from the Disney Store.

***Lion King* fleece throws**

Recently, character fleeces have become increasingly popular. There are quite a few different fleeces available for *Lion King* fans. From left to right are: the Disney Baby Simba plush with his own fleece blanket, a Primark fleece blanket, and an Asda *Lion King* blanket. Primark in particular have been releasing multiple *Lion King* fleece blankets and items in general, as you can see below.

Primark items

Clothing chain Primark have been increasing their Disney lines, and a recurring theme of theirs is none other than *The Lion King*. One of the more prominent releases has a basic yet pleasant pattern, and geared towards adult fans of the movie. Several articles include Timon, Pumbaa and Mufasa (who has probably been mistaken for adult Simba). In addition to this, Primark have also released many other *Lion King* items, such as shirts, pyjamas, wash mitts, Simba onesies, a hot-water bottle cover and more.

Oral-B toothbrushes and toothpastes

Oral-B created a selection of dental hygiene products for *The Lion King*. These included toothbrushes (which feature Simba, Timon and Pumbaa), toothbrush heads and toothpaste.

The Lion King kitchenware

A large variety of kitchenware has been made for *The Lion King*. Thanks to the Disney Store, new kitchenwares are still being made to this day. Above is a selection of kitchenware items. The Pumbaa canteen on the left and the coffee mug on the right are Disneyland Paris releases from *The Lion King* Carnival. The cup with Simba and Nala on the left is a fairly recent retail release, and the cutlery set, Simba face plate and Simba sippy cup are more modern releases from the Disney Store. The other cups, bowl and placemat are regular items from the first movie release.

Aladdin lunchbox and thermos, Happy Ware lunchbox

Here we have a couple of *Lion King* lunchboxes. The one on the left is made by popular lunchbox-maker Aladdin and comes with a thermos (shown here without the lid). On the right is a small lunchbox made by Happy Ware.

The Lion King crazy straws
Straws like these were very popular in the 1990s. Nearly every kid wanted to sip from one, so it's no surprise that SilkJet released a set of *The Lion King* Crazy Straws. The Pumbaa straw is particularly cute and different, in that he's modelled as though he's sliding down the river.

Disney Movie Magic towels
These paper towels were released to help promote the movie's Special Edition release. There were three designs available, before the series continued to another new movie release.

Kleenex and Movie Magic tissues
Much like the paper towels, these tissues were available for a short time to help promote the special edition of *The Lion King*. The set on the right was made by Kleenex, while the box on the left was made by Magic Moments.

Simba telephone
One of the more unusual items, this is a working telephone featuring Simba, released around the time of the original movie's release. It is somewhat clunky, however, particularly when compared to modern mobile phones.

The Lion King clock selection
A selection of clocks. From left to right: Promotional Grolier clock, Simba and Nala clock, and Oh My Disney desktop clock.

Bath gels and soap dish
The Lion King has seen a respectable amount of products made for the bathroom. Shower gels and bubble baths such as the three shown at the back are considered collectible, particularly when they can be doubled as a figure like the ones on the left and right. The middle bottle is more recent, and was only available for a short time. Also shown here is a soap dish featuring Simba and Nala at their own watering hole.

The Lion King promotional freebies

For the original movie's release, Tesco handed out green badges and car stickers with the phrase 'I'm getting my copy of The Lion King from Tesco' alongside Simba (badge) or Simba and Mufasa (car sticker). Since you were allowed to take one at every shop, the badges are uncommon, but the car stickers are very rare these days. Most promotional items for *The Lion King* were released for the Special Edition or Diamond Edition. The two envelopes contain lithographs and were exclusive to Disney Stores. The plastic bag, mug and Simba plush were more promotional items for the Special Edition release.

McDonald's Happy Meal puzzles

Normally I wouldn't include more common items like these, but the bizarre nature of one of them has prompted me to do so. These puzzles were included in McDonald's Happy Meals around the time of the original movie's release. A 'Happy' Meal toy featuring the death of Mufasa? It's almost as though Scar himself approved it.

Simba Activity Ride-on
Made by Kiddieland, this activity ride-on includes several small figures attached. Some fans will prefer to remove the figures to put them on display.

Assorted *Lion King* bags
This is a selection of other bags. From left to right they are: a Disneyland Paris bag with plush Simba keychain, Disney Store sequin bag, Timon and Pumbaa mini pouch clip, and a Lounge Fly tote bag.

Primark bags
Another offering from Primark, shown from left to right are: a laundry bag, backpack, fold-away bag, small bag, and a cosmetics bag.

Older *Lion King* backpacks
You'll find a lot of *Lion King* backpacks out there. Here are a few older ones available from most stores back in the day.

Various *Lion King* stationery items
Stationery items are abundant in the realm of *Lion King* collecting. Shown here is a selection of various stationery items that exist. The mini notepad on the bottom left came from a more recent Disney Christmas cracker. The yellow ruler is an early *Disney & Me* freebie. The remaining items were direct retail releases.

RoseArt collectibles
This is a large selection of the other RoseArt sets that have been released. Since these were usually used by the people that bought them, finding them still in their boxes is becoming increasingly difficult.

RoseArt Deluxe Light-Up Drawing Desk
As seen above, RoseArt released several different arts and crafts items at the time of the first movie. One of these items was a light-up drawing desk, which came with six colouring pages, eight pens and twelve drawing sheets.

The Lion King stationery sets, notebook and barrel pencil case
An assortment of stationery items, from left to right: an eight-piece stationery set, stationery fun set, notepad and a Timon and Pumbaa pencil case. The two in the centre are from the initial movie release, whereas the notepad and eight-piece stationery set are more recent releases.

Boots Lion King Christmas crackers
In 1994, Boots released a set of Christmas crackers for The Lion King. The prizes included figures, stickers, magnets and badges, and the sides of the box featured cut-outs to be used for theatre play. The crackers that can't be seen from the box feature Timon and Rafiki.

Disney Wild Racers
Available both as a double pack and as singular cars, these vehicles, the Pride Land Flyer and Sinister Streetrod, are designed to look just like the siblings from the series. Exclusive to the double pack are the plated cards, detailing information about the racers.

The Lion King MegaBloks items
Megabloks released a few items for the Special Edition DVD release. These items included Megabloks figures featuring Simba, Timon and Pumbaa and a Build with Simba plush toy set that came packaged with some blocks. The company also released a bag of blocks using *The Lion King*'s logo.

Simba (and Mufasa) balloons
Older *Lion King* balloons can be hard to track down, as is to be expected with items this prone to damage. The smaller balloon here is made by Anagram, and was available around the time of the special edition's release. The larger one could be purchased at Disney Parks.

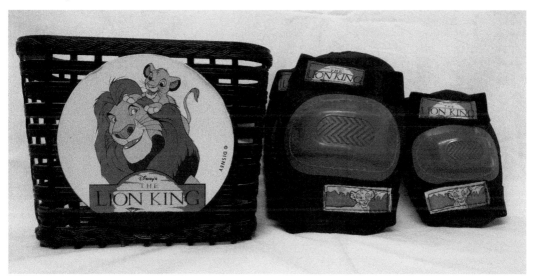

Bicycle basket with knee and elbow pads
Pictured here are a few items for bicycle owners: a basket, elbow pads and knee pads.

The Lion King and Far from the Pride Lands read-along sets

Before the rise of MP3s and even CDs, cassette tapes were the primary source of music on the go. Before companies upgraded to CDs, these read-alongs could be purchased. While the norm for these was a cassette and book combo, some editions came with additional items, such as *Far from the Pride Lands*, which was also released with a Simba watch.

Limited Edition *Lion King* LP

This Special Edition vinyl was limited to 4,000 copies. They were individually numbered at the back of the sleeve. The songs on the LP are the same ones from the original soundtrack.

Collectible tins
These small tins from Disneyland Paris came packaged with candies. Try not to forget the candies inside like I did, because candies that expired twenty years ago can become very sticky...

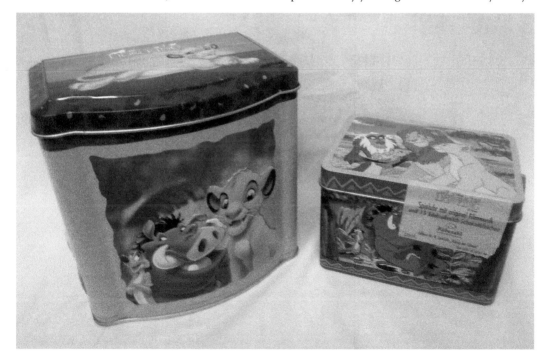

Music box tins
These music tins originally came packed with biscuits. When wound up, a music box rendition of 'Circle of Life' will play.

Intex Inflatable dinghy and ride-on
The most well-known *Lion King* inflatables are the ones released by Intex. Intex created a variety of different inflatable products which included a beach ball, dinghy, Simba ride-on, a rubber ring and more. Later, for the Diamond Edition release of the movie, they released more inflatables, which included armbands, a new Simba ride-on and beach balls. The original items are particularly difficult to locate these days, especially the Simba ride-on. Even the re-release of the ride-on is becoming increasingly popular.

Lion King **plastic balls**
A selection of *Lion King* balls. The first and second from the left are from the original movie release, and the other two were available during the Special Edition release. Locating these can prove a challenge, perhaps because they're fairly easy to pop.

Disneyland Paris food containers

For a while, Disneyland Paris released *The Lion King*-themed packages for their food items. As you could not just walk in and pick most of these up, they became largely throw-away items, since the food items they contained typically ruined the packaging unless removed almost immediately. Not pictured is a paper placemat.

Lion King **snacks**

These items were released for the Special Edition of the movie. The jelly tube doubled as a money bank, and the upright milk chocolate box also contained a small sticker sheet. Also available were the Candy Picpops themselves, but unfortunately these do not seem to survive the test of time very well, since the image becomes obscured by the transparent candy.

Miscellaneous *Lion King* collectibles – wooden pull-along, spinning top and inflatable
An assortment of random items for the fans who want something a little different: a spinning top, light-up spinner toy, Simba and Nala wooden pull-along toys and an inflatable Simba.

The Lion King: A Nature Fun and Learn Series
Also known as *The Lion King: A Nature Fun and Learn Series*, this magazine series lasted an impressive eighty issues in the UK. Each issue came with a free item, usually *Lion King*-themed. Packed with animal facts, *Lion King* stories and African tales, the magazine was very popular. In France, additional issues were also made.

Other *Lion King* magazines
Apart from occasionally being the focus of early *Disney & Me* magazines, *The Lion King* also has other specialised magazines released from time to time. The two on the left are from the ongoing magazine series *Disney Presents*, and the one on the right is from the now defunct *Disney Animated Adventures*.

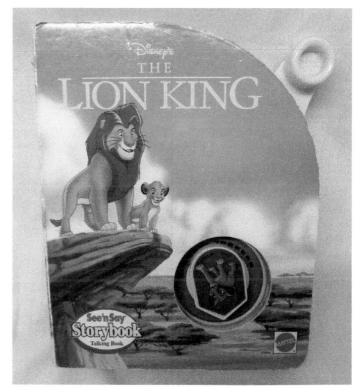

The *Lion King* See 'n Say book
See 'n Say's are collectible even without another brand name. In addition to a regular *Lion King* See 'n Say, a book-format See 'n Say was also produced. A *Simba's Pride* See 'n Say was also released.

The Lion King – six new adventures
This book series is one of the most sought-after items by collectors, due to them only being available via a mail order back before the Internet was widely used, shortly after the release of the first movie on VHS. Although not canon to the movie series, these books follow the story of Simba's son, Kopa, as he learns about the world by hearing stories from others. One book, *A Tale of Two Brothers*, includes the tale of how Scar received his scar and subsequently his name, and is the most popular book of them all. The book series can sell for a good price, but only if you have the original book case as well.

'Friends for Life' cassette
Before we leave Kopa, it's also worth mentioning that he's in two other pieces of media – two German cassette tapes, *Freunde fürs Leben* (Friends for Life) and *Kampf um den Thron* (Fight for the Throne). Despite the cover for both of these tapes relating to the first movie, they take place after it. I believe that both were also released on CD format, but they are much rarer to locate. These were never released outside Germany, so expect to import unless you find a collector willing to sell theirs.

Chapter Two
Simba's Pride

A sequel for what was then considered Disney's biggest success was inevitable, and, after some delays, the movie was released in 1998. In a time when the Internet was still new to many, my first glimpse of *Simba's Pride* was in the now defunct chain of Blockbusters. For fans such as me who had already read *Six New Adventures* long before the sequel was complete, the news of Simba having a daughter was somewhat confusing at first. Yet Kiara turned out to be such a fun-loving character, Kovu's bravery was wonderfully charming and the villains were menacing enough to cause concern for the heroes. While never achieving the same level of popularity as *The Lion King*, *Simba's Pride* is still regarded as one of the better Disney sequels.

Unlike its predecessor, *Simba's Pride* was not quite as heavily merchandised and, like most Disney sequels, it received very little new merchandise after the initial movie release. This has caused *Simba's Pride* collectibles to be much more difficult to locate, and certain items, such as figures or plush toys relating to the two stars, Kovu and Kiara, often reach higher prices compared to *Lion King* collectibles. As before, Mattel was one of the leading suppliers of merchandise for the movie.

Applause and Jemini Kovu and Kiara plush
Much like with *The Lion King*, Applause and Jemini also manufactured some of the more popular *Simba's Pride* plush toys. Featured here are the smaller Kovu and Kiara Applause beanies on the left, and two Jemini plush toys on the right.

Douglas Simba plush
A very rare item indeed, this giant Simba plush by Douglas was available only as a raffle prize at stores such as Asda to help promote the release of *Simba's Pride*. For many collectors, myself included, he is a grail item. (Photography by Lauren Williamson)

Toyworld Adult Simba plush
One of the *Simba's Pride* adult Simba plush toys. Nala is also available. Both of these can be hard to track down. (Photography by Marie Dussol)

Loving Licks Nala plush
These adorable plush toys are made by Mattel. When Nala's back is pressed, her tongue pops out further to lick her cub. Like many smaller items, the Kiara plush is particularly rare, and prone to getting lost. (Photography by Heather Ann Airdrie)

McDonald's Zira plush

If you love the villainous leader of the Outsiders, you'll be disappointed to hear that collectibles featuring her are incredibly limited. Outside of puzzles, boxes and books, these two McDonald's plush toys are the only known items of Zira. The sitting plush is the European release, and the standing plush is the US release.

Outlanders plush set

In the same way that their mother has little attention in the world of merchandise, Vitani and Nuka were similarly shunned where merchandising was concerned. As such, the Outlander plush set by Mattel can reach a good price when sold together. The value rises depending on whether or not the original cardboard tags are present since the artwork on Vitani's and especially Nuka's is highly desirable, particularly as this is the only official artwork of cub Nuka that was ever released.

Pride Landers plush set
Another set was also released for Pride Landers, featuring Kiara, Timon and Pumbaa. This set is not quite as desirable, but completionists will want to add this to their pride.

Trudi Kiara and Kovu plush
These plush toys are made by Trudi, an Italian toy company. They show up from time to time on the secondary market, but this may be because they were also found in crane machines at one point. I won the two in the photo in a claw machine in Hunstanton back in 1999. Timon and Pumbaa were also there, but Kiara and Kovu seemed to be the most prominent.

Giant Kiara and medium Kiara plush
This 3-foot-long Kiara plush was available at the Disney Store and some of the Disney Parks, as was the smaller Kiara plush. A matching Kovu was also released. Finding the larger versions of these plush toys can be difficult, although the smaller variations do come up fairly often.

Medium Kovu and sitting Kovu plush
These two Kovu plush toys are both made by Disney. The smaller one is the companion to the Kiara plush above, while the sitting one is a rarer release. A Kiara is also available in this pose, and is as rare as Kovu.

Kissin' Cubs – Kovu and Kiara
It wouldn't be the same without a release of the Kissing Cubs plush toys. Like before, a magnet in Kovu and Kiara's noses allow them to kiss.

Jemini Kovu pyjama case and Kiara backpack
The Jemini plush backpacks and pyjama cases are incredibly sought-after items, and it's not hard to see why. These collectibles are not only rare, but also one of the more accurate plush toys. Even in a rough condition, these are known to fetch a good price. (Photography by Manon Bouwens)

Mini playsets and assorted Kovu and Kiara figures
Tracking down Kovu and Kiara figures can be somewhat of a challenge. Here, we can see most of the figures that were made. From left to right at the front are: Mattel toddler figures, Mattel figures, Mini Pride Rock Playset, Applause figures, and Thinkway Squeezelite figures. At the back are two Mini Pride Rock Playsets from Mattel. The one on the left is the final product and the one on the right is a prototype packaging. In the centre is a Mattel Mini Collection playset with Kiara stamper. (Photography by Chiara Carchidio)

Simba's Pride Portrait Playcase
Another offering from Mattel, the Portait Playcase interestingly features a cub Simba exterior, and *Simba's Pride* interior. The Kovu and Kiara figures have magnets in their noses, much like the Kissing Cubs plush toys. (Photography by Heather Ann Airdrie)

Bluebird Playset
This playset can be difficult to find with all the pieces included. It's also one of the few collectibles to feature Zira. (Photography by Chiara Carchidio)

Thinkway Timon and Kiara interactive clock
Thinkway Toys produced an alarm clock which interacted wirelessly with a very specific Kiara plush. The pair will work together to set up an alarm for you during those important days. Of course, you can use them alone, but it's not much fun.

***Simba's Pride* bed set**
For the release of *Simba's Pride*, Disney Store UK released a set of items for the perfect *Simba's Pride* themed bedroom. These included a duvet and pillow, valence sheet, headboard (which itself is a rarity) and more. Also available in this series are matching curtains, a lampshade, metal bin, small lamp and storage boxes.

Simba's Pride beanbag
A beanbag from the above series, using the same pattern.

Foldable bed
One of the more unusual items from the franchise as a whole, this foldable bed can be changed into a chair for easy storage use.

Simba's Pride rug
This rug is technically part of the above set, but features a completely different pattern.

Simba's Pride Disney Classics mug
This is the only known mug from the Disney Classics range which features *Simba's Pride*.

Simba's Pride placemat, glasses and melamine plate
A few pieces of cutlery were released for *Simba's Pride*, but these items are much more difficult to find, especially when compared to *The Lion King* cutlery items.

Kiara bubble bath figure, plus Kiara and Kovu sponges
Here we have a couple of sponges featuring Kovu and Kiara plus a bubble bath container which doubles as a rather impressive figure/statuette.

Simba's Pride promotional items
Simba's Pride saw a variety of items that came free with purchase or pre-order, depending on where it was purchased. Some of these items included an orange yo-yo, a small black backpack, a lithograph and decorated envelope set, and a colour-your-own t-shirt.

Simba's Pride GameBreak and variations
A surprisingly enjoyable PC game for all ages (but marketed towards younger players), the *Simba's Pride* GameBreak includes several mini games that can be played alone or with a friend. There exists a regular disc and a brown printed disc, which contains a couple of additional files (that don't impact gameplay). The mini-games have been re released on several discs, often as standalone games. The brown disc is the rarest edition.

Simba's Pride Activity Centre and variations
Known as *Simba's Pride* Active Play in the US, this Activity Centre included several mini games, and seven unique songs that can also be heard when inserting the disc into a CD player. It was re-released on a number of occasions. One release, a *Daily Mail* giveaway, erroneously uses art and information from the GameBreak instead. The original big box edition is the rarest.

The Lion King: Simba's Mighty Adventure GameBoy Colour and PlayStation games
The Lion King: Simba's Mighty Adventure tells the tale of Simba from the very beginning of the first movie, up to the end of *Simba's Pride*. The game itself is enjoyable, but far less challenging than the original console game. The PlayStation also includes clips from both movies.

Simba's Pride **stationery set**
The Disney Store pencil holder set shown here came packaged with a notepad, Kovu eraser and a pencil. The other sides of the pencil holder feature Kovu and Kiara with the same expression as shown on the notepad, and Timon and Pumbaa. The notepad was also available with other items.

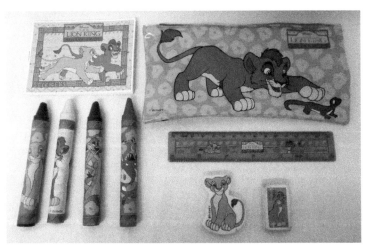

Assorted *Simba's Pride* stationery
A selection of assorted stationery items from *Simba's Pride* were produced, including a pencil case, ruler, Kovu eraser, Kiara eraser, four crayons and a mini sticker book.

Simba's Pride Edu-kit

Clementoni are known for releasing Edu-kits for several franchises, and *The Lion King* is no exception. The *Simba's Pride* mini Edu-kit is considerably rarer than most other Edu-kits that have been released for the franchise.

Backpack

Backpacks such as these can be quite difficult to locate in a new condition. This particular backpack also comes with a small pouch and a set of pencils.

Kiara and Kovu helmet
This is a rare helmet featuring Kiara and Kovu. This doesn't show up very often for sale.

Puzzles
Here we have a couple of puzzles. Since it's rare to see adult Kiara, adult Kovu and Zira, these could be considered an interesting find for fans.

Miscellaneous items

A selection of miscellaneous items: play ball, memory card games (same game, different boxes), two mini puzzles, Decofun wallpaper border and *Simba's Pride* lollipop holder, which strangely uses cub Simba as the figural holder.

Assorted items

A selection of assorted items: Kovu wallet (which was also available in green), *Disney & Me* door plate, two badges, a birthday card from Disneyland Paris which allows you to change the age from three to fifteen (a rare case for *Simba's Pride*, since other merchandise was typically aimed towards youngsters only), and a large Anagram Kiara balloon.

Chapter Three
The Lion King 3

It's no secret that Timon and Pumbaa brought about the most laughs. Using their signature motto *Hakuna Matata,* meaning 'No Worries', the meerkat and warthog duo were hugely successful, and a plethora of merchandise followed in their wake.

In 1995, the best friends received their own television show, known as *The Lion King's Timon & Pumbaa.* Although the episodes typically centred around the friends themselves, a few episodes also focused on Zazu, Rafiki or the hyena trio. The series lasted for three seasons, with a total of eighty-five episodes, though merchandise dedicated to the show was minimal.

Much later, in 2003, the pair became the stars of the next *Lion King* movie – *The Lion King 3: Hakuna Matata* (or as it's known in America, *The Lion King 1½: Hakuna Matata*), a midquel film detailing the events which led to Timon finding Pumbaa and their involvement in the events of the first *Lion King* film. The movie was essentially a parody, which differed greatly from the original story of Timon's past that was explained in *The Lion King's Timon & Pumbaa.* Although the movie was successful, it also divided fans.

Merchandise for the movie was even slimmer than that of *Simba's Pride.* Some items that were released in the UK would drop the '3' from the title and branded items with *The Lion King* name instead.

Timon and Pumbaa LCD game
Timon and Pumbaa also received their very own LCD game by Tiger. Players could call Simba to help them with certain enemies.

Timon and Pumbaa's Jungle Games (GameBreak) and variations
Also available for the Super Nintendo, GameBreak (sometimes referred to by its other name, *Timon and Pumbaa's Jungle Games*) included several mini games, including a pinball game and Puyo Puyo-style game. Some of the mini games were re-released in different packaging.

Adventures in Typing with Timon and Pumbaa
As the name suggests, this educational game was aimed at teaching kids to type. For those able to complete all of the challenges, a song found nowhere else would be played, sung by Timon and Pumbaa, titled 'It's Good to Be Home Again'. The song was not uploaded to the Internet until 2014, which probably shows just how few people actually made it to the end.

Big Time Comic featuring The Lion King's Timon and Pumbaa
UK magazine *Big Time* would often feature Timon and Pumbaa in some way. This also included comics.

The Lion King GameBoy Advance game
While marketed in the UK as *The Lion King*, in the US the GameBoy Advance game was correctly labelled as *The Lion King 1½*. The UK title is thus misleading, since the gameplay focuses on the third movie rather than the first.

Bandai *Pumbaa Siesta*
Created by Bandai, players must remove bugs which a rotund Pumbaa (or 'Pumba' as he is referred to here) carries in his tree trunk base, without having him wake up.

Timon and Pumbaa tumbler, plate and bowl set
This set contains a plate, cup and bowl. It's interesting to note that the design used on the bowl is the same one seen on *Simba's Pride* merchandise.

Promotional Pumbaa beanbag
This promotional plush was given out to those who purchased the movie for a limited time.

Pouncin' Action Mufasa and Simba
This Hasbro figure set was released in the US, but I've found that this and other figures in the series tend to crop up in the UK every now and then. Also available are Fight to the Finish Simba and Scar, Bowlin' Action Timon and Pumbaa (which also comes with Shenzi, Banzai and Ed). (Photography by Heather Ann Airdrie)

Hasbro figure sets (Photography by Chiara Carchidio)
Despite featuring in the movie, merchandise of Ma and Uncle Max is rather dire. During the release of the movie, Hasbro released small three-figure sets: Circle of Life, containing Timon, Pumbaa, Mufasa, Sarabi, Rafiki with baby Simba, a zebra and a gorilla; Simba's Adventure, containing cub Simba, cub Nala, Scar, Zazu, Banzai, a giraffe and an ostrich; and finally Jungle Fun, which contained Ma and Uncle Max, plus reprints of cub Nala, cub Simba, Timon, Pumbaa, Rafiki with baby Simba and Banzai.

The Lion King 1½ sneak peek booklet
The little booklet pictured here was a bonus for those ordering *The Lion King Special Edition* in the US. Not only did it contain savings on a number of items (primarily *Lion King*), it also contained a diary that was written by Timon, detailing all the events from the day he left his home to the day Simba reclaimed his kingdom. According to the booklet, the events from Simba's presentation to Simba's return took place over the course of roughly a year (provided, of course, that you consider this movie canon).

Chapter Four
The Lion Guard

To celebrate *The Lion King*'s 25th anniversary in June 2014, an announcement by Disney revealed a new upcoming series based off the hugely successful franchise – *The Lion Guard*. The series would include a short introductory movie and a television series that would follow later. This extension takes place during *The Lion King* and *The Lion King II: Simba's Pride*, and chronicles the adventures of Simba's son, Kion, and his Lion Guard, a group dedicated to protecting the Pride Lands from danger. His team, consisting of Bunga the honey badger, Fuli the cheetah, Beshte the hippo and Ono the egret, are the first Lion Guard in the Pride Lands' history not to be comprised fully of lions.

The pilot, *Return of the Roar*, quickly became the highest-viewed program on Disney Junior, with over five million viewers during its premiere. With Just Play and Disney Store taking the reins for the merchandise, the series was off to a great start, but somewhere during the second half of the first season, an erratic schedule saw fans waiting months just to watch a single new episode. By the time the Season 2 special, *The Rise of Scar,* had aired in the USA, the show had started to receive significantly less advertising and merchandise had become increasingly difficult to find. Not too long after the fifth wave of blind bag figures had been released, Just Play silently halted production of the merchandise, only making it known when concerned fans started to contact them on social media. Following this, the majority of upcoming book releases for the show were also cancelled unceremoniously.

The Lion Guard blind bag figures

Created by Just Play and released in January 2016, *The Lion Guard* blind bag figures were a huge hit for the series, including figures of several characters that otherwise had no other toys made. The figures spanned a total of five waves over a period of two years and were distributed in Europe by Simba, and in the UK by Flair from Wave Two onwards. Sadly, the UK never saw an official release of the first wave. That being said, Wave Five, the final set, was only released in the UK. Each series contained a number of normal figures, plus one special edition figure with a metallic coating. Some waves included reprints of figures found in earlier series, meaning the only figures not released at any point during the UK are standard Fuli, Janja and Golden Kion.

Although there is no verbal mention of which character is in each packet, it is still possible to detect which figure you will receive by analysing the code at the back of the pack. These numbers are usually tied to the model, meaning a metallic figure will share the same code as the regular figure. For example, Wave One Fuli is 06, and the Wave Four metallic Fuli (shown here on the far left) is also 06. Some characters also had two codes, for example, a Wave Five Kovu can be found in 042 and 503 packets.

The Lion Guard Pride Land Brawlers

The Lion Guard Pride Land Brawlers was one of the first pieces of merchandise released. These electronic figures will interact with each other when placed close enough. Later, Just Play also released non-electronic versions of these figures which saw a limited release around the world, but also included Fuli and Janja. A stock photo of an electronic Fuli has been spotted, but has seemingly been cancelled.

The Lion Guard Battle Pack with accessory

The Lion Guard Battle Pack figure sets, created by Just Play and distributed by Flair, are often sought after by collectors, purely for the villain figures included. For a long time these were the only villain figures available on the market, until Just Play began to re-release some of them in other sets and the blind bag figures saw more waves released. Despite this, no other Makuu figure was ever made. An Ono set, which came with his launcher and the same Janja figure from Kion's set, was released exclusively by Simba Toys in Europe.

The Lion Guard poseable figures

The Lion Guard poseable figures were one of the last items available on the market before Just Play ceased making merchandise for the show. Despite the name, only one of the figures in each pack is poseable. A third set which included Fuli and Janja was never released in the UK, and a second wave of figures was cancelled.

Disney Store *Lion Guard* plush toys

The Disney Store released a set of plush toys for *The Lion Guard*, including the Guard themselves, their arch enemy, Janja, and Timon and Pumbaa (not shown here, which used the same patterns as their previous toy, just with a new tag). Later, Makini joined the team, before she was even seen on the show. In her limited run, she was available with two tags (shown here with the first release).

Zuru Lion Guard **capsule figures**

Zuru released a set of capsule figures. These blind box-style toys were not quite as blind as you might believe. Much like the blind bag figures, you can tell what figure will be in each capsule by the colour of the bottom line. Kion's band is brown, Bunga's is blue, Ono's is green, Fuli's is yellow and Beshte's is gray.

Training Lair playset
Measuring over 3 feet tall, the Training Lair Playset retailed for £69.99 at launch. Also included are a standard poseable Kion figure and Janja figure.

Rise of Scar playset
First shown at Toy Fair 2016, the Rise of Scar playset immediately caused fans to speculate over Season 2 of *The Lion Guard*, after hearing that Scar would be returning. When Scar's nose is pressed, his eyes and the flames around him light up while he roars. This is the only playset to include a (partial) figure of Kiburi.

Posh Paws plush (Wave One)

The Posh Paws plush toys are rather infamous in the collector community for being off-model, especially in comparison to other toys available on the market. The first wave consisted of Kion, Bunga, Fuli, Ono and Beshte, who were also available in beanie forms. Kion, Bunga and Ono also received large versions, and Fuli was available in this size in other European countries. Keychain plush toys were also released in Europe.

Posh Paws plush (Waves Two and Three)

Wave Two comprised Kion (who received embroidered eyes for this release), Fuli (whose eyes were also updated), Simba, Kiara, Timon and Pumbaa. Beanie versions were also available. Wave Three contained only Janja, who was also later released as a keychain plush in Europe.

The Lion Guard **bath toy set**

The set of bath toys is known for being very cute and for having two very obvious mistakes printed on two of the figures. On Fuli, her Mark of the Guard is printed over her old circle (which, in the show is removed upon receipt of her Mark of the Guard) and on Kiara her eyes are strangely green instead of her usual brown. Two odd mistakes for a product created by none other than Disney themselves!

The Lion Guard Vtech InnoTab game
With apps on the rise, *The Lion Guard* InnoTab game is the only physical video game made for the series. As the box may suggest, it includes a variety of games aimed at educating children on various subjects.

The Lion Guard magazine
Compared to *The Lion King*'s magazine series, *The Lion Guard* magazine did not last for quite as long, spanning a total of fourteen issues plus two preliminary issues that were part of the *Disney Presents* magazine. Each issue contained various facts on animals, a poster, free items (which were sometimes repeated) and a unique comic found only in these magazines (excluding a French release of the earlier comics in hardback format). Although released in multiple countries, the UK magazine lasted the longest. In Germany, a special edition blind bag containing a Golden Roaring Kion was also included in issue three.

The Lion Guard night light puzzle ball

Ravensburger created several puzzles for *The Lion Guard*, but the Nacht-Licht (Night Light) Puzzle Ball is probably the most interesting. Once created, it can be used as either a regular puzzle ball or transformed into a night light with a bright or dim light, which can be controlled by a simple hand clap or by the switch underneath.

Protect the Pride Lands, Matching Game and Boulder Burst games

An assortment of board games were created by Wonder Forge: Protect the Pride Lands (which strangely contains figures of Kion, Bunga, Beshte and Fuli, but no Ono), Matching Game and Boulder Burst.

Quizzy, Pop-up Game and Surprise Slides games

A selection of other *Lion Guard* games include Quizzy, Pop-up Game and Surprise Slides (known in the US as Roaring Rescue).

91

The Lion Guard 16-inch bicycle
Since we've showcased a few bicycle items here, it seems only right that we feature an actual bicycle. This bike, created by Italian company Dino Bikes, was released shortly after the television show began airing in the UK. It was available in 12-inch, 14-inch and 16-inch sizes.

Lion Guard activity kits and pencil case
The most well-known stationery items featuring *The Lion Guard* cast were made by Disney themselves and were sold exclusively at Disney Stores. Shown here are two activity cases and a pencil case which includes several pens.

Assorted *Lion Guard* kitchenware items
As a show geared towards pre-schoolers, *The Lion Guard* was heavily merchandised in the kitchenware department. Shown here is a selection of various items. All but the breakfast set and cutlery set on the right were exclusive to the Disney Store.

The Lion Guard event items

During the initial release, Disney hosted a few events across the UK. Most of these took place in Disney Stores, and one was hosted at Westfield Stratford. Shown here are the prizes given out at Disney Stores – a certificate and sticker sheet. Finding them mint can be difficult, since these were usually written on by staff and the stickers were handed out separately. The other item shown here is a card that was available at Westfield Stratford. Since there's a special promotion at the back, many of these were handed in at Disney Stores to take advantage of the offer.

Chapter Five
Musical

The musical production first appeared in 1997. The UK production has been at the Lyceum Theatre for over seventeen years, and enjoys continued success. In fact, in 2014 *The Lion King* became the top-earning title in box office history for both stage productions and films, surpassing *The Phantom of the Opera*. The musical offers a few differences from the movie, including some scenes that were deleted from the original movie release.

Baby Simba Musical plush
One of the larger and more popular gifts you can buy, this baby Simba plush is jointed. He measures around 13 inches when standing.

***The Lion King* Musical bracelet, limited edition ornament and mug**
The lightweight ornament also features the name of the city it was purchased in on the back (in this case, London). The mug comes with a handy spoon. The set of charming bracelets features authentic beads and designs, including baby Simba's portrait, Mufasa's face (the logo of the musical) and Pumbaa.

I first visited the show around a year after it was released, when my school had a coach trip organised. Watching it as a child was as magical as watching the movie (despite our coach driver getting lost in London, causing us to miss the 'Circle of Life' performance). Yet now, even as an adult, whenever I make the trek up to London to watch the show it brings tears to my eyes with its spectacular performances.

In terms of merchandise, there's always a good selection of items to purchase before and after the show. The items are usually more souvenir related such as plush toys, mugs and cups, bags, apparel, stationery, towels, CDs, jewellery and of course programmes. What merchandise is on offer varies depending on when you visit, and some items that were previously out of stock may be restocked in the future.

The Lion King Musical cup, flag and paper bag
Shown here is a paper bag that was available with purchase of any item, a plastic cup that could be purchased only with a drink, and a promotional mini flag.

Assorted Lion King Musical items
Here are some smaller items: a pencil case, a truck, plastic keychain, metal keychain, plastic magnet and metal magnet.

Chapter Six
The Future

The Lion King seems to show no signs of slowing down anytime soon, with the CGI remake movie now on the horizon. With a trailer that reached a staggering 224.6 million views within the first twenty-four hours, the love for this inspirational franchise looks promising. *The Lion King & Jungle Festival* will also celebrate the movie's release at Disneyland Paris, so fans of all ages can once again celebrate this wonderful franchise. There is also a Season 3 of *The Lion Guard* coming that will hopefully explain Kion's whereabouts during the events of *Simba's Pride*.

There is bound to be ample new merchandise that will be produced from a variety of different companies for many years to come. Regardless of your collecting focus, Disney seem to be keeping the flame going for almost every category, ensuring many more collecting adventures for fans in the great circle of life.